Real Size Science

Materials

Rebecca Rissman

Raintree is an imprint of Capstone Global Library Limited, a company incorporated in England and Wales having its registered office at 7 Pilgrim Street, London, EC4V 6LB – Registered company number: 6695582

www.raintreepublishers.co.uk
myorders@raintreepublishers.co.uk

Edited by Rebecca Rissman, Daniel Nunn, and John-Paul Wilkins
Designed by Joanna Malivoire and Tim Bond
Picture research by Ruth Blair
Production by Sophia Argyris
Originated by Capstone Global Library Ltd
Printed and bound in China by South China Printing Company

ISBN 978 1 406 26348 0 (hardback)
17 16 15 14 13
10 9 8 7 6 5 4 3 2 1

ISBN 978 1 406 26355 8 (paperback)
18 17 16 15 14
10 9 8 7 6 5 4 3 2 1

British Library Cataloguing in Publication Data
Rissman, Rebecca.
Materials. – (Real size science)
620.1'1-dc23
A full catalogue record for this book is available from the British Library.

Acknowledgements
We would like to thank the following for permission to reproduce photographs: Shutterstock pp. 4 wood (© Natali Glado), 4 metal (© michaket), 4 rock (© Dervin Witmer), 5 rubber (© Emin Ozkan), 5 glass (© STILLFX), 5 plastic (© Ambient Ideas), 6 (© Marie C Fields), 7 (© irakite), 8 (© Marta Tobolova), 9 (© mrsnstudio), 10 (© vasi2), 11 (© Joe Hamilton Photography), 12 (© Robert Hoetink), 13 (© Payless Images), 14 main (© Pawel Nawrot), 14 inset (© Peter Gudella), 15 (© Blazej Lyjak), 16 (© LacoKozyna), 17 (© hempuli), 18 (© Stepan Kapl), 19 (© WimL), 20 (© panda3800), 21 main (© Olivier Le Moal), 21 inset (© ungureanu), 22 (© Losevsky Photo and Video), 23 ornament (© sauletas).

Cover photograph of a tree trunk reproduced with permission of Shutterstock (© mythja).

We would like to thank Dee Reid and Nancy Harris for their invaluable help in the preparation of this book.

Every effort has been made to contact copyright holders of material reproduced in this book. Any omissions will be rectified in subsequent printings if notice is given to the publisher.

Contents

Materials

There are different types of materials.

wood

metal

rock

rubber

glass

plastic

paper

5

Everything we use is made from materials.

Things made from materials
can be different sizes.

Plastic

Plastic can be a hard, shiny material. These toy bricks are made from plastic.

Real size

Plastic can be a flexible material.
This rope is made from plastic.

Metal

Metal can be a heavy material.

This hammer is made from metal.

Real size

Real size

Metal can be a light material.
This tin foil is made from metal.

Glass

Glass can be a hard material.

This windscreen is made from glass.

Glass can be a fragile material. These ornaments are made from glass.

Rubber

Rubber can be a stiff material.

Car tyres are made from rubber.

Real size

Real size

Rubber can be a flexible material.
Shoe soles are made from rubber.

Rock

Rock can be a dull material.

These bricks are made of rock.

Real Size

16

Rock can be a shiny material. The diamond in this ring is a type of rock.

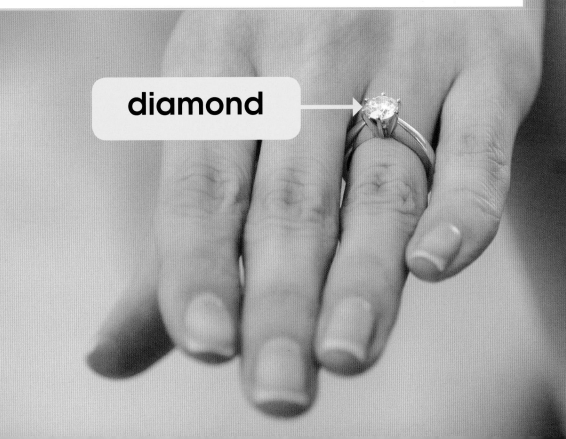

diamond

Wood

Wood can be a soft material.

We can cut into wood.

Real size

Wood can be a hard material.
This mallet is made from wood.

Paper

Paper can be a flexible material.
This crane is made
from paper.

Real Size

Paper can be a stiff material.

This cardboard is made from paper.

Real size surprise!

This tiny skateboard is made from plastic.

Real size

Picture glossary

 **flexible** bends or moves easily

 **fragile** easy to break

 **ornament** something that is nice to look at

Index

Notes for parents and teachers

Before reading
- Tell children that all things are made of materials. There are different types of materials, such as metal, wood, glass, rock, plastic, rubber, and paper.
- Write material names on the board, and then encourage children to brainstorm different items made from those materials.
- Explain to children that objects made from materials can be big or small. Tell children that we can use tools, such as rulers, to measure size. We can also use body parts, such as hand lengths and foot lengths, to measure size.

After reading
- Ask children to turn to pages 16–17. Compare and contrast the paving stone on page 16 with the diamond on page 17. Which is larger?
- Ask children to think of three objects made from wood. Then ask them to rank these objects in order of size.